TUNDRA

Published by Willow Creek Press, Inc.
P.O. Box 147, Minocqua, Wisconsin 54548

Printed in China

TUNDRA

BEARS IT ALL!

CHAD CARPENTER

◫ WILLOW CREEK PRESS®

18

45

47

48

49

54

60

POOH LEARNS THE HARD WAY WASPS DON'T MAKE HONEY

WHY IS IT IF WE RIP UP A CAMPSITE OR EAT A FEW HIKERS, WE'RE CONSIDERED TO BE **ROGUE BEARS**? IS IT REALLY TOO MUCH TO JUST WANT OUR FEELINGS VALIDATED?!

The Official Short but Sweet Bio of Chad Carpenter

Having no other marketable talent, Chad decided to take a crack at a life-long ambition of being a newspaper cartoonist. The year was 1991 and he had just moved back to his home state of Alaska after living in Sarasota, Florida for three years. It was while in Sarasota that Chad became greatly inspired and personally advised by two of the comic strip greats - Mike Peters (Mother Goose & Grimm) & Dik Browne (Hagar the Horrible).

Shortly After arriving back in Alaska, armed with little more than 36 sample strips, a whole lot of ignorance and a burning desire to avoid real work, Chad went to the Anchorage Daily News to pedal his wares. The features editor took one look at "Tundra" and said "Eh, maybe we'll give it a try."

Fortunately, they actually did.

Shortly after the Daily News started running TUNDRA, it was picked up by most of the other Alaskan newspapers. A year later Chad was able to quit his job as a process server/security guard and devote all of his energy to being a cartoonist.

After 15 years of being only in Alaska newspapers, TUNDRA broke loose on the rest of the world.

In just five years, TUNDRA has added almost 500 newspapers including the L.A. Times, the Seattle Times, the Denver Post, the Pittsburgh Post, the San Francisco Chronicle as well as newspapers throughout Europe, Jamaica & Trinidad.

In May of 2008 Chad was presented with the Reuben Award for "Best Newspaper Panel" by the National Cartoonist Society.

Chad currently lives in Wasilla, Alaska with his wife Karen and four children. He is busy working on his 21st book as well as the latest calendars, shirts, greeting cards and anything else he can make a buck on.